Introduction to EARTH'S RESOURCES

HOW WE GET
FOOD

Nancy Dickmann

Crabtree Publishing Company
www.crabtreebooks.com

T0014879

Crabtree Publishing Company
www.crabtreebooks.com

Author: Nancy Dickmann
Editorial Director: Kathy Middleton
Editor: Ellen Rodger
Picture Manager: Sophie Mortimer
Design Manager: Keith Davis
Children's Publisher: Anne O'Daly
Proofreader: Debbie Greenberg
**Production coordinator and
  Prepress technician:** Ken Wright
Print coordinator: Katherine Berti

Photographs (t=top, b=bottom, l=left, r=right, c=center)
Front Cover: All images from Shutterstock
Interior: Aljazerra: Katrina Yu 11; iStock: Marie Art 7, B4lls 25,
S Bayram 15, Sera Ficus 5, fishwork 6, JGaunion 14, Kall9
9, Monkey Business Images 23, Anastasia Nurullina
29, HM Proudlove 8, SDI Productions 17, yusnizam 16;
Public Domain: Dag Enressen 27; Shutterstock: Benjamin
Photography 22, Marius Dobilas 13, Roman Drotyk 4, FenlioQ
10, Yein Jeon 24, Ben Petcharapiracht 26, Ratckova 18, Joshua
Resnick 28, smereka 12, BG Smith 19, Sunshine Seeds 21,
YuRi Photolife 20.
All facts, statistics, web addresses and URLs in this book
were verified as valid and accurate at time of writing. No
responsibility for any changes to external websites or
references can be accepted by either the author or publisher.

Library and Achives Canada Cataloguing in Publication

Title: How we get food / Nancy Dickmann.
Names: Dickmann, Nancy, author.
Description: Series statement: Introduction to Earth's resources |
  Includes bibliographical references and index.
Identifiers: Canadiana (print) 20200284436 |
  Canadiana (ebook) 20200284460 |
  ISBN 9780778781875 (softcover) |
  ISBN 9780778781813 (hardcover) |
  ISBN 9781427125996 (HTML)
Subjects: LCSH: Food—Juvenile literature.
Classification: LCC TX353 .D53 2020 | DDC j641.3—dc23

Library of Congress Cataloging-in-Publication Data

Names: Dickmann, Nancy, author.
Title: How we get food / Nancy Dickmann.
Description: New York : Crabtree Publishing Company, 2021. |
  Series: Introduction to earth's resources | Includes index.
Identifiers: LCCN 2020029723 (print) | LCCN 2020029724 (ebook) |
  ISBN 9780778781813 (hardcover) |
  ISBN 9780778781875 (paperback) |
  ISBN 9781427125996 (ebook)
Subjects: LCSH: Food--Juvenile literature. |
  Nutrition--Juvenile literature.
Classification: LCC TX353 .D53 2021 (print) | LCC TX353 (ebook) |
  DDC 641.3--dc23
LC record available at https://lccn.loc.gov/2020029723
LC ebook record available at https://lccn.loc.gov/2020029724

Crabtree Publishing Company
www.crabtreebooks.com   1-800-387-7650
Published in 2021 by Crabtree Publishing Company

Copyright © Brown Bear Books Ltd 2020

Published in Canada
Crabtree Publishing
616 Welland Ave.
St. Catharines, ON
L2M 5V6

Published in the United States
Crabtree Publishing
347 Fifth Ave
Suite 1402-145
New York, NY 10016

Printed in the U.S.A./082020/CG20200710

Contents

We Need Food!

There are more than 7 billion people in the world. What do we have in common? We all eat food!

Food is anything that you eat to give you **energy** and keep your body going. The human body uses food as a fuel, the same way that a car uses gas. Being active burns up this fuel. Then you must eat more food to replace the energy that you've used up.

The energy in food is measured in calories.

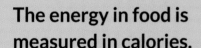

An apple has about **90 calories**.

The average 9-year-old needs about **1,700 calories** per day.

A healthy meal includes whole grains and plenty of vegetables.

The harder your body works, the more food you burn.

A Healthy Diet

The kind of foods you eat matters a lot. Foods all have different **nutrients**. These are things the body needs to survive and grow. Some nutrients help build strong bones. Others provide energy or keep your blood healthy. A healthy, balanced diet includes many different foods.

Growing Crops

A lot of the foods we eat are plants. They are often grown on farms.

Plants that are grown for food are called **crops**. Rice, corn, and wheat are types of grain. They are some of the most common crops. Farmers also grow fruits and vegetables. Even drinks like tea and coffee are grown as crops on large farms.

Farming plants is one of the world's major industries.

More than **40%** of the world's calories come from just three crops: rice, wheat, and corn.

About **11%** of all the land on Earth is used for growing crops.

Chocolate comes from a plant called cacao that is grown by farmers.

Once you plant a seed, it takes about three months for a corn plant to be ready to harvest.

On the Farm

Many crops are grown in large fields. The farmer plants seeds and then waters the plants as they grow. Once the plants are fully grown, they are **harvested**. The parts we eat, such as the grains on a stalk of wheat, are separated from the rest of the plant.

Raising Animals

Many people eat meat. The animals that provide meat are raised on farms.

Long ago, people hunted animals to eat. Many people still do this, but most meat now comes from farms. Farmers raise cows, pigs, chickens, sheep, and goats. Some farms raise ostriches or bison! Farmers feed and take care of the animals until the animals are ready to be eaten.

Large numbers of animals are raised on farms around the world.

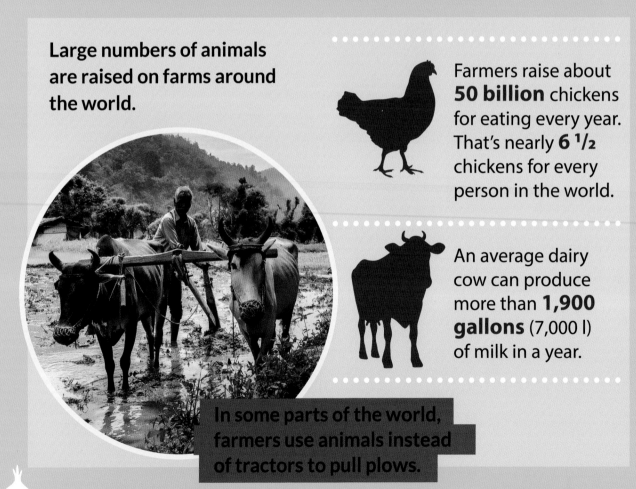

Farmers raise about **50 billion** chickens for eating every year. That's nearly **6 1/2** chickens for every person in the world.

An average dairy cow can produce more than **1,900 gallons** (7,000 l) of milk in a year.

In some parts of the world, farmers use animals instead of tractors to pull plows.

More than Meat

We raise farm animals for other reasons too. Cows and other animals, such as goats, produce milk. We drink milk and also make it into cheese, ice cream, and yogurt. Chickens and ducks produce eggs, and bees make honey.

Farmers raise shrimp, salmon, and other seafood on fish farms.

Where in the World?

Food is produced all over the world. Different foods are grown in different places.

Not all plants are the same. Some grow best in dry conditions. Others need plenty of rain. Different regions of the world have different **climates**. They are each suited to different kinds of plants. Apples grow well in cooler areas, while pineapples and bananas need a warmer climate.

Rice grows well in damp soil that has plenty of water.

It takes about **300 gallons** (1,100 l) of water to produce just **1 pound** (0.5 kg) of rice.

Some potatoes are made into french fries, which are popular in many countries.

Going Global

Different crops had their start in different regions. Once, tomatoes and potatoes grew only in South America. Turkeys came from North America. Then explorers brought these foods back to Europe, Asia, and Africa. Now these crops are grown and eaten around the world.

About **170 million tons** (154 million metric tons) of tomatoes are grown each year. China grows **31%** of the world's tomatoes.

Food Factories

We eat some crops just as they are, such as bananas. Other foods are sent to factories to be made into something else.

Factories use farm products as ingredients. They might make milk and chocolate into ice cream. They can grind wheat or corn into flour, then use it to make bread, pasta, tortillas, and even breakfast cereals. Factories mix different ingredients to make sauces, cookies, soups, and more.

Factories have machines that can quickly turn crops into other products.

About **69%** of wheat flour is used to make bread and bread products such as bagels or muffins.

Preserving Food

Some factories process food so it lasts longer. They might freeze fresh fruits and vegetables such as berries and peas. They put fruits, vegetables, and soup into cans. These foods will still be fine to eat months later. Factories **preserve** meat by smoking, salting, drying, or canning it.

Most canned foods last for 1 to 5 years.

Putting foods into cans, jars, and boxes makes it easier to ship and store them.

Growing Bigger, Growing Smarter

Today's farmers use technology. It helps them grow bigger and better crops.

Farmers use machines to plow the land and plant seeds. They have systems for watering crops. They use chemicals to kill weeds and insects, and to help the plants grow better. Farmers who raise animals use technology too. There are machines for feeding animals and milking cows.

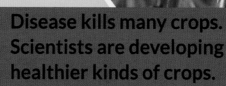
Disease kills many crops. Scientists are developing healthier kinds of crops.

In China, insects destroy **11%** of the rice crop each year. In India, it is **18%**.

The temperature inside a high tunnel is warmer than the temperature outside.

Using Science

Scientists have come up with ways for farmers to get more out of their land. They use greenhouses and **high tunnels** to grow plants in cooler climates. They test the soil to find out which nutrients should be added. They develop new and better versions of the plants they grow.

Greenhouses and tunnels cover about **22,000 square miles** (57,000 square km) of land around the world.

Thank You, Bees!

Farmers depend on more than just technology to grow crops. They rely on insects too!

Most food plants need to be pollinated. This means taking a dusty material called **pollen** from one flower to another. The pollen is needed for the plants to grow fruits and seeds. Sometimes pollen is blown where it needs to go by the wind. But more often, it is taken by bees.

Farmers bring beehives to their fields when the crops need pollinating.

Around the world, insects pollinate about **$170 billion** worth of crops each year.

Bees are dying off fast. In some places, numbers of bees have gone down by **90%**.

The pollen sticks to hairs on a bee's body.

Brushing Off

Bees visit flowers to drink a sweet liquid called nectar. As the bees drink, pollen brushes onto their bodies. When they fly to another flower, the pollen brushes off. This pollinates the flower. If there were no bees, farmers would have to pollinate some crops by hand. This would be difficult and expensive.

Keeping Land Healthy

Crops need water, air, and sunlight to grow. They need nutrients too.

Nutrients are chemicals in the soil that help keep plants healthy. When plants grow, they take nutrients out of the soil. If farmers want to use the same field over and over, they must replace the nutrients that have been used up. Spreading **fertilizers** on fields is one way to do this.

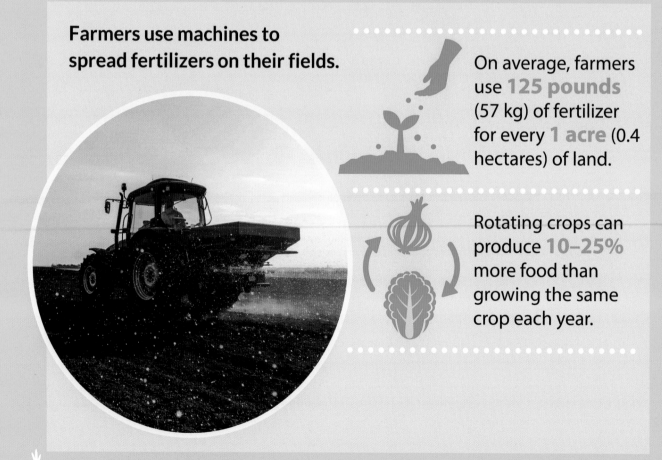

Farmers use machines to spread fertilizers on their fields.

On average, farmers use **125 pounds** (57 kg) of fertilizer for every **1 acre** (0.4 hectares) of land.

Rotating crops can produce **10–25%** more food than growing the same crop each year.

Putting Nutrients Back

Some fertilizers are made in factories. Others come from animal waste. Fertilizers replace nutrients in the soil. Farmers also rotate, or switch, which crops they grow. Different crops need different nutrients. Growing the same crop over and over can use up all of a certain nutrient in the soil. Switching crops from year to year helps keep the soil healthy.

Some crops, such as peas, actually put nutrients back into the soil!

Farming Problems

Farms produce the food that we need to survive. But farming can also cause problems.

There are more people in the world than ever before. That means we need more food to feed everyone. People sometimes cut down forests to grow crops or raise animals. This destroys **habitats** where wild animals live. Farming can also damage the soil. Without care, soil can dry out and blow away.

Rain forests are being cut down to make space to grow plants such as oil palm.

Between 1990 and 2016, **502,000 square miles** (1.3 million square km) of forest were cut down. That's about twice the size of Texas.

Scientists are trying to breed cattle that produce less methane.

Climate Change

Some gases in the atmosphere trap heat, making Earth's temperature rise. This is called global warming. It is changing climates around the world. **Carbon dioxide** and **methane** are two of these gases. Trees help reduce carbon dioxide in the air because they absorb it. But cutting down forests gets rid of helpful trees.

There are about **1.5 billion** cattle in the world. Each one produces up to **264 pounds** (120 kg) of methane per year.

Food Shortages

Sometimes there is not enough food for people to eat. This can happen for many reasons.

Bad weather can damage crops. If there is not enough rain, or too much rain, plants may die. Insects or disease can also damage them. Even if crops grow well, they don't always get to the people who need it. Wars and natural disasters can cut off supplies. Some people just don't have enough money to buy the food they need.

Huge swarms of insects called locusts can quickly eat entire fields.

In 2019 swarms of locusts destroyed **40%** of the crops in Pakistan.

Charities and governments help provide food for people who need it.

Not Enough Food

When a person doesn't get enough food, it is called **malnutrition**. This is a serious condition. People with malnutrition often lose weight and become weak. Their bodies have a harder time fighting off illnesses. Even people who eat enough food sometimes don't get enough of certain nutrients. This can cause health problems.

Throughout the world, about **462 million** people are underweight due to malnutrition. This includes **52 million** children under five years old.

Food Miles

How does food get from the farm to your plate? Sometimes it has to go on a long journey!

Many areas produce a lot of their own food. It doesn't have to travel far. But some foods, such as pineapples or chocolate, can only be grown in certain places. Other foods only grow during the summer. In winter, they must be grown in greenhouses or shipped in from warmer places.

Fleets of trucks, trains, and airplanes carry food around the world.

About **70%** of food in the United States travels by truck. About **4.5%** goes by air.

In the United States, **20%** of all food is imported, or brought in, from other countries.

Fresh fruits and vegetables spoil quickly, so they are often shipped by airplane.

Food from Far Away

Food miles are the distance that food has to travel before it is sold. Food can be shipped by truck, train, boat, or airplane. All of these vehicles release carbon dioxide into the atmosphere. This gas makes the planet warm up. Shipping food by airplane costs a lot, and it releases the most carbon dioxide.

A single meal can have ingredients from many different countries.

Wasting Food

We aren't always careful with food. A lot of it gets wasted.

There are many reasons why food gets thrown away instead of eaten. Food producers often get rid of fruits or vegetables that are the wrong size, or a funny shape or color. Stores throw away food that is close to its **expiry date**. People at home throw away leftovers or unused food such as bread that has gone stale.

Food waste often ends up buried in a landfill, or dump, with other trash.

In North America, the average person wastes about **250 pounds** (113 kg) of food in a year.

About one-third of all food is wasted. This is about **1.4 billion tons** (1.3 billion metric tons) per year.

Packaged food is labeled with a date that shows when it is past its freshness.

Using Waste

Some of the wasted food gets thrown away. But food waste can be useful! It can be collected in a pile to break down into compost. Compost is a kind of fertilizer that helps crops grow. It can also be broken down in special machines. As it breaks down, it releases a gas. The gas is collected to use as a fuel.

What Can I Do?

Food is a precious resource. Here are some tips on how you can protect it.

- Plant bee-friendly flowers in your garden to provide food for bees.

- Check to see where the food you buy comes from. Try to buy food that is grown closer to home.

- Producing meat and dairy releases a lot of methane. Try to eat more vegetables and less meat.

- Don't waste food! Buy only what you need to cook the meals you plan. Use up old food before buying more.

- Collect vegetable peelings and other food scraps to recycle into compost.

Quiz

How much have you learned about food? It's time to test your knowledge!

1. What are the three most common crops in the world?

a. tea, coffee, and chocolate

b. rice, corn, and wheat

c. raspberries, strawberries, and blueberries

2. How much milk can a cow produce in one day?

a. 5 tablespoons

b. 5 glasses

c. 5 gallons

3. What substance do bees carry from flower to flower?

a. honey

b. pollen

c. glitter

4. What happens inside a food factory?

a. crops are grown indoors

b. fake foods are made from plastic

c. food is preserved or made into other food products

5. Where do tomatoes and potatoes originally come from?

a. South America

b. Australia

c. Mars

Answers on page 32.

Glossary

carbon dioxide A gas found naturally in the air, which is also produced when we burn fuels

climates The average weather patterns in areas over a long time

crops Plants that are grown for food

energy The ability to do work

expiry date A date by which a food product needs to be sold, so that it is still fresh when it is eaten

factories Buildings where products are made or put together

fertilizers Chemicals that help crops grow better

food miles The distance that food travels between where it is produced and where it is used

habitats The natural homes of animals or plants

harvested To have cut or picked plants when they are ready to eat

high tunnels Tunnels made of hoops covered in thin plastic; used to grow fruits and vegetables

malnutrition A condition in which the body doesn't get enough of the nutrients that it needs

methane A gas that traps heat in the atmosphere

nutrients Chemicals that a person, animal, or plant needs to grow and stay healthy

pollen A substance produced by flowers that helps them make seeds

preserve To treat a food so that it will last longer without spoiling, such as by freezing or canning it

Find out More

Books

Brannon, Cecelia H. *Corn* (All About Food Crops). Enslow Publishing, 2017.

Chancellor, Deborah. *Don't Waste Your Food* (Good to Be Green). Crabtree Publishing, 2020.

Leaf, Christina. *Honeybees* (Insects Up Close). Bellwether Media, 2017.

Small, Cathleen. *How Plants Grow* (Let's Find Out!). Rosen Educational Publishing, 2018.

Websites

https://challenge.ivaluefood.com
This month-long challenge has tips on how to cut down on food waste.

https://kidstir.com/where-food-comes-from-game/
This interactive game shows children where their food comes from.

www.dkfindout.com/uk/animals-and-nature/plants/plants-as-food/
Learn how plants have been grown as food crops for thousands of years.

Index

Quiz answers

1. b; 2. c; 3. b; 4. c; 5. a